PUNCH

PUNCH

by Colleen Mullaney

Photographs by
Jack Deutsch

CHRONICLE BOOKS
SAN FRANCISCO

Text copyright © 2005
BY COLLEEN MULLANEY

Photographs copyright © 2005
BY JACK DEUTSCH

Library of Congress Cataloging-in-Publication Data available.

ISBN 0-8118-4177-4

Manufactured in China.

Distributed in Canada by Raincoast Books
9050 Shaughnessy Street
Vancouver, British Columbia V6P 6E5

10 9 8 7 6 5 4 3 2 1

Chronicle Books LLC
85 Second Street
San Francisco, California 94105

www.chroniclebooks.com

PROP STYLING BY *Laura Maffeo*
DESIGNED BY *Tracy Sunrize Johnson*

CONTENTS

6 **Introduction**
7 History Lesson
8 Punch Basics

15 **Fruity Concoctions**
16 Nantucket Lemonade
19 Fruit Smoothie
20 Petal Punch
23 Raspberry Rambler
24 Sunrise Surprise
27 Melon Melody
28 Papaya Pleaser

31 **Old Standards**
32 Bloody Mary Bowl
35 Sassy Sangria
36 Holiday Ho Ho
39 Mulled Cider
40 Gin Rummy
43 Julep Jubilee
44 Minty Mojito
47 Orange Crush
48 Pimm's at Play

51 **Tropical Paradise**
52 Margarita Madness
55 Citrus Cooler
56 Dockside Delight
59 Paradise Found
60 Mango Tango

63 **Champagne Wishes**
64 Peachy Passions
67 Pink Lady Punch
68 Fruity Bubbles
71 Tangerine Dreams
72 Afternoon Delight
75 Mimosa Punch
76 Love Train

79 **Coffee, Tea & Lemonade**
80 Coffee on the Cubes
83 Rose Hip and Hibiscus
   Tea Punch
84 Ginger Tea Punch
87 Fruited Tea Punch
88 Old-Fashioned Lemonade
91 Sparkling Mint and
   Strawberry Lemonade

92 **Basic Recipes**

94 **Index**

96 **Table of Equivalents**

PUNCH: *It's like a party in a bowl!*

Once a staple at events like showers and holiday gatherings, then relegated to the ranks of passé trends, punch is again finding favor on the party scene, enjoyed by the young and hip as well as hosts and their guests from every corner. Today's style setters seem to be taking a step back from the fast track and embracing entertaining as their parents once did— surrounding themselves with the company of family and friends and serving up some homemade fun.

Punch, so easy to make and with a retro-hip air of nostalgia, is the perfect solution to the dilemma of wanting to entertain but being short on time. Because let's face it: though we like nothing better than to be social, we're all busy people, and more and more it seems that there aren't enough hours in the day to get life's necessities under control, much less think about entertaining. So, what to do? Make things simple, beginning with the beverages. Why mix, stir,

pour, and serve a dozen drinks when you can make a great time with one punch?

There are really no rules to punch making. Anyone who can stir with a spoon can concoct a batch of punch; all that's needed is a bowl, a few choice ingredients, and someone to share in the imbibing. The art lies in the choosing of those ingredients to make a harmonious hooch, so I undertook a study of punch. Rummaging through Mom's recipe collections yielded punch recipes for all occasions, from casual get-togethers and impromptu cocktail gatherings to bridal showers and intimate dinners. From twists on the classic favorites to fun and contemporary inventions, this book represents many hours of tasting, testing, changing, and updating those old recipes— and the creation of many new ones based on the lessons learned. With punch, it all depends on what you pour in and the parts making up the whole, so read on and find the perfect mix for your next party.

HISTORY LESSON

Punch dates back to the 1600s. By many accounts the name comes from the Hindu word *panch,* meaning "five," presumably after the ingredients that were first used in the mix: lime, sugar, spices, water, and a fermented sap called arrack (an ancestor of rum.) The English got their first taste of what would soon become the darling drink of the Empire sometime around 1655, after their conquest of Jamaica. British sailors evidently took a liking to the cooling beverage, often making mention of it in their journals and letters home from sea.

By the eighteenth century, punch had become very popular among the British upper classes, and was even seen as a status symbol. Rum was still one of the main ingredients, but other liquors such as bourbon and brandy began to find their way into the mix. Always a celebratory drink, serving punch became a mark of social and economic standing. No household of means was without a cut-crystal punch bowl, and the bigger the better.

Soon, what began as a summery island fruit drink found its way to the cooler climates of the early North American colonies, where it was usually mixed with milk, cream, wine, or hot water and served all year long. There, its status grew from mainstay to heyday, as in the 1940s and 1950s, when it became the standard offering at weddings, showers, and other celebrations that called for something special, eventually to such a ubiquitous degree that it more or less wore out its welcome within the contemporary cocktail aesthetic. Though never truly abandoned, punch continued to wane in popularity during the 1980s and 1990s, reduced it seems to occasional appearances at group events or simply a term for fruit ades for children.

Today punch is experiencing a second honeymoon. This quintessential celebratory drink with wide appeal is reemerging as a refreshing change from wine, beer, and the usual mixed drinks. Party givers everywhere are dusting off their mothers' or grandmothers' crystal bowls and cups and experiencing the pleasures of punch.

PUNCH BASICS

LIQUOR LESSONS

While some think bottom shelf when they think punch liquors, assuming the fruit flavors and mixers will conceal the lesser quality of the spirit, this is not always so. I would urge always to choose a good brand. It doesn't have to be the most expensive or top shelf, but something in between will assure adequate flavor and smoothness. For wine punches, choose wines that you would drink on their own, rather than budget jug wines.

BRANDY

Distillates from wine or other liquors, this large family of spirits is best known for its high-quality versions Cognac and Armagnac.

GIN

Gin is made with a grain base infused with juniper berries and a variety of other herbs and spices.

LIQUEURS

Liqueurs are liquors that have been diluted, sweetened, or flavored with fruits, herbs, and/or spices. Often intense and fairly heavy, liqueurs fall halfway between wine and hard liquor in alcohol content. They are enjoyed for sipping and in many cases are used in cooking. Typically a liqueur is defined by one flavor element, for example hazelnut in amaretto, orange in Cointreau, and black currant in crème de cassis.

RUM

One of the world's oldest liquors, rum is made from sugarcane molasses in the islands of the Caribbean and South America. Rums range from clear to dark brown in color, each with a distinct flavor. (For further rum reading, see page 19.)

TEQUILA

Made from the heart of the agave plant, tequila is distilled into several different types classified according to the number of years they are aged: the youngest, or freshly distilled, are blanco (white) or plata (silver), the "rested" resposado is aged at least 2 months in oak barrels or casks, and the ultrasmooth and sipping

tequila, anejo, has been aged at least a year. I like to use 100 percent agave in punch for the best flavor.

VODKA

Distilled from either potatoes or grain, vodka has traditionally been the province of Eastern or Northern Europe, but now brands are even popping up from potato fields on eastern Long Island.

WHISKY

This grand liquor family encompasses Scotch whisky, blended Scotch, Irish whiskey, Canadian whisky, bourbon, rye, and sour mash. The wide range in flavor and in proof is the result of different methods of distilling and the variety of grains used.

BOWLS, GLASSES, *and* LADLES

Nowadays, punch bowls come in many forms. The basic thing to keep in mind is that as long as a bowl or container has ample space for holding the mix, it is a fine punch bowl. Search your cupboards and use your imagination, or commit to punch and buy a new bowl. Even "official" punch bowls are versatile vessels; you're sure to find many uses.

In the past, silver, fancy etched or engraved glass, or cut-crystal bowls were de rigueur for punch—and always with matching glasses. Today, rules for entertaining a crowd permit for a variety of creative containers. For instance, if you're entertaining in the garden, why not use a flower bucket? On Derby Day, a silver trophy cup makes a perfect punch bowl. Bowls can be glass, plastic, metal, or ceramic; it all depends on the type of gathering and the practical demands of the setting. I once made punch for a moving party in a plastic mop bucket. The punch was thoroughly enjoyed by everyone, and once empty, the bucket, along with brushes and a mop, became the housewarming gift.

There is an infinite selection of good punch glasses out there, and you probably have more than a few in the cupboard. An acceptable punch glass has but few requirements. Since punch can be a pretty potent libation, stay away from large goblets and water glasses. Any glass that holds approximately 8 ounces of punch will do. This includes juice glasses, wineglasses, jelly jars, old-fashioned glasses, and small tumblers. If you can, gather Champagne glasses for the bubbly punches and margarita glasses, Irish coffee cups, or silver julep cups for those specialty punches. In general, don't worry if you don't have a set of eight or twelve matching glasses; I mix and match a variety of styles and colors and find it contributes a touch of fun and whimsy to the presentation.

I purchased a good portion of my glassware collection at tag sales, thrift shops, and warehouse-style housewares stores. I continue to add to my collection over time and am always amazed at the different styles and colors of glasses to be had. If you already have an eclectic collection of glasses, now is the perfect time to use them.

There's not much to say about the ladle, but it is a tremendously important tool for punch presentation. The alternative, of course, is dunking the glasses, which makes for quite a sticky mess. Metal, plastic, glass, or wood, ladles are good choices for scooping up the punch, and all are readily available at housewares stores.

GARNISHES

Garnishes can be the finishing flavor touch, and of course are always a visual key to the punch's presentation. I remember my grandmother never let drinks be served without olives or fruit. With punch garnishes, you can create big effects with little effort. Colorful herb leaves, fruit slices, and berries make terrific garnishes. Flowers—petals or buds—also make a strikingly pretty detail. There is a wide variety of edible and other pesticide-free flowers available in markets today (usu-ally packed in small plastic containers

and prewashed to make them ready to use). A few colorful and sturdy types to look for are marigolds, nasturtiums, roses, and pansies. Incorporate them into ice cubes or molds, float them freely in the punch bowl, or use them to garnish glasses.

The sweetest of common herbs, mint is a widely used garnish in punch, and I've used it in many of the recipes that follow. Mint is easy to find or to grow and is available in many different scents, and in addition to spearmint and peppermint, there are heady varieties such as lemon and chocolate mint. All add their own spice and flavor to the punch recipe, so experiment with what's available.

Thin fruit slices such as orange, lemon, lime, peach, and pineapple and whole frozen berries like raspberries, cranberries, blueberries, strawberries, and blackberries make for tasty and colorful additions to punch, either frozen in ice, floating freely in the bowl, or bedecking individual glasses. Markets today carry a wide vari-ety of fresh fruits year-round, so try to find fresh before frozen, and don't be afraid to go tropical—grab some mango or papaya and garnish away!

DECORATIVE ICE CUBES
and ICE FORMS

Ice cubes and other ice forms not only keep the punch nicely chilled, but when filled with bits of fruit, berries, flower petals, or herb leaves add an eye-catching and impressive touch to a simple recipe. Common as water itself, the classic ice cube becomes jewel-like when enhanced with a decorative center. Ice cube trays are also now available in shapes from stars to sea horses, bringing whimsy to ice without the extra step of freezing in a garnish.

Ice molds are available in a wide assortment of shapes and styles. The traditional large ice rings allow lots of space for adding flowers, herbs, or fruits, but can prove cumbersome to guests as they are ladling away. The elegant look of a classic ring may warrant any fuss for some, but also consider the smaller rings and other shapes, which won't clog up the bowl, as they can move about freely. Ice molds can be found in the baking sections of kitchen stores or in the candy-making aisle of your local crafts store. Improvised options include milk cartons or yogurt containers that have been emptied and washed, or soup bowls or ramekins from your pantry.

Whatever shape or mold you choose, be sure the ice is frozen solid to avoid a watery result, and place it in the punch at the last minute before guests arrive. At average room temperature, large ice forms will usually last 3 to 4 hours, smaller ones 2 to 3 hours, and ice cubes about an hour. If you're serving punch outside on a hot day, be well prepared, as ice will disappear quickly. As the ice melts, instead of adding more cubes to the punch itself—as this will water down the recipe—put cubes in a separate bucket for guests to fill their glasses before ladling up the punch.

For instructions on how to make decorative ice cubes and other forms, see page 92. Feel free to use these in any recipe calling for plain cubes; likewise, if time doesn't permit, you can replace molded ice in a recipe with ice cubes.

TIPS *for* PERFECT PUNCH

✿ Chill all punch ingredients, especially juices, nectars, and carbonated mixers, before making the punch.

✿ When possible, use fresh lime and lemon juice (as the recipes call for) to add extra zest. Simply roll the fruit, cut in half through the middle, and use a press or juicer to release the fresh juice. For juices that require larger quantities, such as orange and grapefruit, store-bought juices will save you time in the kitchen.

✿ Add all carbonated beverages such as ginger ale, sparkling water, and Champagne to the punch last to ensure bubbles when serving.

✿ Place the punch bowl out of direct sunlight to preserve the ice and keep a cool serving temperature.

✿ Fruit nectars or juices such as papaya, passion fruit, and mango can be found in the international food aisles of well-stocked grocery stores or in specialty-foods markets.

✿ When serving large crowds, double or triple the recipe depending on the number of people you are expecting. Always taste the recipe after adding each ingredient as you may find nectars and fruit juices do not have to be added in full quantities. Refrigerate the mix to keep it well chilled until ready to use. If the recipe includes a carbonated beverage or Champagne, add these, along with any ice, just before serving.

FRUITY CONCOCTIONS

Fruit is a natural place to start with punch bases, given the realm of drinkable flavors and infinite recipe possibilities. When available, always use fresh fruit rather than frozen, as fresh fruit has a lower water content. Nowadays, there is a plethora of seasonal and/or exotic fresh fruits, such as raspberries, papaya, and mango, that can be found year-round in grocery stores or specialty-food markets along with once hard-to-find nectars such as passion fruit and guava. But when fresh isn't available, frozen works just fine; just look for fruit that has been frozen in its own juices and not in sugary syrup that can take the sweetness of the punch over the top.

NANTUCKET LEMONADE

This punch gets its name from a concoction I whipped up for a dockside get-together on the island several summers ago. The ginger ale balances the tart lemon and lime citrus tones, while the cranberry juice adds sweetness and vivid, festive color. After all, if you're going to name a drink after one of the cranberry capitals of the world, the juice should star.

Punch bowl and glasses
5 cups lemonade, homemade (page 88) or good-quality purchased
2 cups cranberry juice
3 tablespoons fresh lime juice
3 cups vodka
2 cups chilled ginger ale
4 cups ice cubes
Frozen cranberries and lemon slices for garnish

Combine the lemonade, cranberry juice, lime juice, and vodka in the punch bowl and mix well. Just before serving, slowly pour in the ginger ale. Add the ice cubes. Garnish with the frozen cranberries and lemon slices and serve immediately.

SERVES 12

✴ For nonalcoholic Nantucket Lemonade, substitute 2 cups additional ginger ale and 1 cup additional cranberry juice for the vodka.

NOTE: *For a picnic or harbor cruise, mix the punch directly in a small insulated cooler for instant and easy transportability.*

FRUIT SMOOTHIE

This is a true favorite among my friends. This is a sweet punch, perfect for brunch or springtime gatherings. The homemade fresh raspberry puree gives a velvety texture to the mix, but if you're short on time, you can use raspberry syrup, found in well-stocked supermarkets, instead.

Punch bowl and wineglasses

2 cups Raspberry Puree (page 93) or **$^1/_2$ cup** raspberry syrup (see Note, page 23)
6 cups pineapple juice
2 cups orange juice
2 tablespoons fresh lemon juice
3 cups light rum
4 cups ice cubes

Combine Raspberry Puree and the other liquid ingredients in the punch bowl and mix well. Add the ice cubes and serve immediately.

SERVES 12

✳ For a nonalcoholic Fruit Smoothie, substitute an additional 3 cups pineapple juice for the rum.

NOTE: *You'll notice that the recipes in this book specify either light or dark rum. Clear "light rum," also called white or silver rum, is the lightest and most preferred for mixed cocktails and punches, as the flavor blends but does not overpower the fruit juices and other ingredients. Rich brown-colored dark rum, made from molasses, is used for cocktails where a more pronounced rum flavor is desired, as it has a stronger taste.*

PETAL PUNCH

This zingy punch is perfect for balmy summer afternoons. It has a subdued fruity flavor, but if you wish to turn it up a notch, add ripe, sweet seasonal fruits such as nectarines (my favorite), peaches, strawberries, or raspberries.

Punch bowl and glasses
24 ice cubes made with rose petals (see page 92)
Two bottles (750 ml each) chilled Zinfandel or rosé wine
2 cups cranberry juice
1 cup orange juice

At least 3 hours ahead, make the rose petal ice cubes.

Combine the liquid ingredients in the punch bowl. Add the ice cubes and serve immediately.

SERVES 12

RASPBERRY RAMBLER

Festive doesn't even begin to describe this party pleaser packed with very-berry flavor. This one is a great summer sipper—with a kick! Mix up a batch for the after-beach cool down, and wait your turn in the shade for the outdoor shower.

Punch bowl and glasses
Ice form(s) made with lime slices and raspberries (see page 92)
1 1/2 cups Raspberry Puree (page 93) or **1/2 cup** raspberry syrup (see Note)
4 cups pineapple juice
2 cups vodka
1/2 cup fresh lime juice
3 cups chilled orange-flavored sparkling water
Lime slices and raspberries for garnish (optional)

At least 3 hours ahead, make the ice form(s).

Combine the Raspberry Puree, pineapple juice, vodka, and lime juice in the punch bowl and mix well. Just before serving, slowly pour in the sparkling water. Place the ice form in the punch. Garnish with the lime slices and raspberries, if desired.

SERVES 12

✳ For a nonalcoholic Raspberry Rambler, substitute 2 cups pineapple juice for the vodka.

NOTE: *Raspberry syrup is available at specialty-food stores and well-stocked supermarkets.*

SUNRISE SURPRISE

Skip the coffee; this punch is a definite eye-opener. Great for breakfast or brunch, the mango and passion fruit flavors add an exotic fresh fruit taste. This delicious wake-up call not only brings out the best of the morning, it's packed with vitamin C! You can find the tropical juices at international food markets and well-stocked supermarkets.

Punch bowl and glasses
3 cups pineapple juice
2 cups mango juice or nectar
2 cups passion fruit juice or nectar
1 cup orange juice
2 $^1/_2$ cups light rum
$^1/_2$ cup Cointreau
$^1/_2$ cup apricot brandy
6 cups ice cubes
Orange slices for garnish

Combine the liquid ingredients in the punch bowl and stir well. Add the ice cubes, garnish with the orange slices, and serve immediately.

SERVES 12

For a nonalcoholic Sunrise Surprise, substitute an additional 2 $^1/_2$ cups orange juice for the rum.

MELON MELODY

Reminiscent of a fancy martini, this sexy drink is perfect for a gathering of friends. The colorful garnishes, made of tiny fresh melon balls, are easy to make and add an impressive finishing touch. But be forewarned, the melon soaks up the punch, so be careful snacking!

Punch bowl and glasses
4 cups pineapple juice
2 cups vodka
3/4 cup Midori (melon liqueur)
1/2 cup cream of coconut (see Note)
1/2 cup fresh lime juice

1/2 small cantaloupe, chilled
1/4 small honeydew melon, chilled
1-inch-thick slice of small seedless watermelon, chilled
4 cups crushed ice

Mix all of the liquid ingredients in the punch bowl.

Cut the melons into 1/2-inch balls using the smaller end of a melon baller. Thread the melon balls in combinations onto 8 large cocktail picks or small skewers. If you have more melon than you need, cut additional balls and float them in the punch for added color.

Add the crushed ice to the punch. Garnish individual glasses with the melon ball swizzles and serve immediately.

SERVES 8

NOTE: *Cream of coconut, not to be confused with the unsweetened coconut milk and cream used for cooking, is a thick, sweetened coconut product found in liquor stores and well-stocked supermarkets.*

PAPAYA PLEASER

This bright orange punch has the divine taste of the tropics and is sure to delight a crowd. The papaya has a commanding but subtle, sweet taste and smoothes out the rum kick, making this a drink to please almost anyone.

Punch bowl and glasses
Ice form(s) made with lemon slices (see page 92)
5 cups papaya nectar
2 cups pineapple juice
2 cups light rum
¹/₂ cup fresh lemon juice
¹/₂ cup dark rum
Kiwi or lemon slices for garnish (optional)

At least 3 hours ahead, make the ice form(s).

Combine all of the liquid ingredients in the punch bowl and mix well. Place the ice form(s) in the punch and serve immediately. Garnish the punch bowl or the glasses with the fruit slices, if desired.

SERVES 10

✳ For a nonalcoholic Papaya Pleaser, substitute 2 cups additional pineapple juice for the rum.

OLD STANDARDS

This chapter features classic punches and others based on cocktails that have been crowd pleasers over the years and are still going strong with today's social set. So, get nostalgic for the old while mixing up a batch of punch for your generation of swell partygoers.

BLOODY MARY BOWL

The old standby for breakfast, brunch, or afternoon gatherings. The addition of lime juice adds extra citrus freshness while dousing the hot and spicy flavors a bit. I leave the bottle of hot sauce next to the punch bowl for those more willing to fire up their senses. This punch version of the Bloody Mary is full flavored and, some say, the perfect hangover cure.

Punch bowl and glasses
12 lemon wedges
12 lime wedges
12 large pitted olives
8 cups tomato juice
3 cups vodka
3/4 cup Worcestershire sauce
1/2 cup fresh lemon juice

1/4 cup fresh lime juice
1/4 cup prepared horseradish
2 teaspoons hot red pepper sauce
1 teaspoon freshly ground black pepper
1 teaspoon celery salt
8 cups ice cubes
6 celery stalks, trimmed
    and cut in half lengthwise

Thread 1 lemon wedge, 1 lime wedge, and 1 olive onto each of 12 cocktail picks or small skewers. Set aside. (These colorful garnishes can be made up to 1 day ahead and kept in the refrigerator, covered with a damp paper towel.)

In the punch bowl, whisk together the tomato juice, vodka, Worcestershire sauce, lemon and lime juices, horseradish, hot pepper sauce, black pepper, and celery salt. Add the ice cubes. Garnish each glass with a celery stalk and citrus-olive swizzle and serve immediately.

SERVES 12

✱ For a nonalcoholic Virgin Mary bowl, simply omit the vodka.

SASSY SANGRIA

Sangria is the punch that's perfect anytime. It's easy to make and the results are not only colorful but lively and full flavored, with the citrus tang of lime and orange complementing the wine's dryness. A traditional quaff that's rapidly becoming one of the drinks of the moment, sangria is being offered everywhere from tapas restaurants to the sidelines at polo matches to buffet tables at pool parties.

Pitcher and glasses

Two bottles (750 ml each) chilled
dry red wine such as Zinfandel,
Merlot, or Pinot Noir

2 cups orange juice

$^3/_4$ cup Cointreau

$^1/_4$ cup fresh lime juice

2 to 3 oranges, thinly sliced

2 to 3 limes, thinly sliced

2 to 3 lemons, thinly sliced

2 cups chilled sparkling water

4 cups ice cubes

Combine the wine, orange juice, Cointreau, lime juice, and fruit slices in the pitcher and mix well. Refrigerate for at least 30 minutes or up to 2 hours to allow the flavors to marry. Just before serving, slowly pour in the sparkling water. Add the ice cubes and serve immediately.

SERVES 12

✱ Variation: For a sangria with a little kick, add about $^3/_4$ cup brandy to the mix; just be sure to use a smooth, mellow brandy and taste as you go so as not to overpower the sangria's fruity flavors, avoiding a revolution in the bowl.

> **NOTE:** *Sangria is a wine punch that derives from the French drink* sangaree, *which is sweetened wine with spices, typically nutmeg, and sometimes fruit juice. The Spanish version is a chilled punch made of red or white wine mixed with brandy, fruit juice, sugar, and soda water. Both words come from the Latin word for blood,* sanguis, *a reference to the deep crimson color of the punch.*

HOLIDAY HO HO

*What better time than the holidays to indulge in a decadently rich beverage?
Our version of the classic egg nog, an essential part of holiday celebrations over the
years, is particularly potent; reduce the amount of bourbon and brandy, if you like.
This heavenly holiday beverage can be made up to 1 hour ahead and refrigerated
before serving.*

Punch bowl and glasses
24 eggs, separated
2 cups sugar
1 cup bourbon
2 cups brandy
4 cups heavy cream

8 cups whole milk
1 quart good-quality
   vanilla ice cream, softened
2 tablespoons vanilla extract
Freshly ground nutmeg for sprinkling

In a large bowl, using an electric mixer, beat the egg yolks and sugar until
thick. Add the bourbon and brandy and mix to combine thoroughly. The liquor
will "cook" the eggs. Add the cream and milk and continue beating while
adding the ice cream in small amounts until combined. Stir in the vanilla
extract.

In another bowl, with clean beaters, beat the egg whites until stiff. Fold into
the ice cream mixture. Pour into the punch bowl, sprinkle with nutmeg to
taste, and serve.

SERVES 12

* For nonalcoholic Holiday Ho Ho, omit the bourbon and brandy and add
2 teaspoons each ground nutmeg and cinnamon.

MULLED CIDER

There's nothing like drinking something warm on chilly autumnal days. This punch, with its soft spice tones, is great after a football game or trick-or-treating. Serve it from the front porch as you watch the Halloween parade go by.

Large earthenware or insulated serving bowl and mugs or glasses
10 cups apple cider
5 cinnamon sticks, plus more for garnishing glasses (optional)
About 40 whole cloves
12 orange slices
2 teaspoons ground ginger
1 teaspoon freshly ground nutmeg
3 small apples

In a large saucepan, combine the cider, cinnamon sticks, 10 of the cloves, 6 of the orange slices, the ginger, and the nutmeg. Bring to a boil, then reduce the heat and simmer for 25 minutes. Meanwhile, stud the apples with the remaining cloves.

Strain the spiced cider into the serving bowl. Garnish with the clove-studded apples and remaining orange slices and serve. Tuck fresh cinnamon sticks in individual glasses, if you like.

SERVES 10

✱ Variation: To really take the chill out, add 2 cups of bourbon just before serving.

GIN RUMMY

This yummy gin punch is light enough to serve before a big holiday dinner. Replace the club soda with tonic and you've got yourself a warm-weather party pleaser. This recipe ranked number one at one of many punch-tasting parties for this book.

Punch bowl and glasses
3 cups gin
1$\frac{1}{2}$ cups orange juice
1 cup apricot brandy
8 cups chilled club soda
6 cups ice cubes
3 limes, thinly sliced
3 lemons, thinly sliced
2 tangerines, thinly sliced

Combine the gin, orange juice, and brandy in the punch bowl and mix well. Just before serving, slowly pour in the club soda. Add the ice cubes and fruit slices, reserving some of the fruit slices to garnish individual glasses if desired. Serve immediately.

SERVES 12

✳ For a nonalcoholic Gin Rummy, omit the brandy and substitute an additional 3 cups of orange juice for the gin.

JULEP JUBILEE

Serve a bowl of this refreshing classic to friends on Derby Day and you'll see the bets increase as the afternoon goes by. Although the recipe calls for 100-proof bourbon, 80-proof would do just fine.

Large silver punch or other serving bowl and julep cups or heavy glasses
1 cup mint-flavored Simple Syrup (page 93), cooled
4 cups 100-proof bourbon
1 cup loosely packed fresh mint leaves, plus more for garnish
8 cups crushed ice

Chill the serving bowl and glasses in the freezer for at least 1 hour.

Combine the Simple Syrup and bourbon in the serving bowl and mix well. Add the 1 cup of mint leaves and crushed ice. Garnish individual cups with mint leaves and serve immediately.

SERVES 12

* You can also garnish the cups with nontoxic flowers such as camellia or roses (see page 11).

A SOUTHERN TRADITION *A true emblem of the South, the mint julep originated in either Maryland or Virginia and originally had as its main ingredient either brandy, rum, or rye. But with its migration to the South, specifically Kentucky, bourbon became the star player. Here the glass the drink is served in is just as important as what's inside; silver cups are part of the julep tradition and, when chilled, take on the perfect, alluring frostiness.*

MINTY MOJITO

A classic Cuban drink, the mojito has quickly become the most popular drink on the social scene in recent years. Serve with plantain chips, salsa, and cigars. Take a sip and float away to tropical Havana.

Punch bowl and glasses
4 cups light rum
1 cup mint-flavored Simple Syrup (page 93), cooled
$^1/_2$ cup fresh lime juice, preferably from Key limes
6 cups crushed ice
2 cups chilled sparkling water
1 cup loosely packed mint sprigs, plus more for garnish
3 limes, preferably Key limes, thinly sliced

Combine the rum, Simple Syrup, and lime juice in the punch bowl and mix well. Just before serving add the crushed ice and slowly pour in the sparkling water. Garnish individual glasses with lime slices and mint sprigs. Add the remaining mint sprigs and lime slices to the punch and serve immediately.

SERVES 12

* Variation: Add $^1/_4$ cup lemon juice to the punch for a dash more of citrus delight.

ORANGE CRUSH

A retro favorite, this punch is ideal for game night. The flavor is a mix between orange soda and Creamsicle pops. If you have truly modern taste buds, use orange sorbet instead of sherbet, although the sherbet has a creamy texture that would be missed. Serve with cocktail franks, deviled eggs, or Swedish meatballs; just ask Mom for the recipes.

Punch bowl and glasses
4 cups chilled orange soda
$2^1/_2$ cups vodka
$^1/_2$ cup Cointreau
1 quart orange sherbet
Orange slices for garnish

Combine the orange soda, vodka, and Cointreau in the punch bowl and mix well. Just before serving, carefully spoon the sherbet into the bowl; it will fizz and foam as it starts to melt. Garnish with the orange slices and serve immediately.

SERVES 10

* For a nonalcoholic Orange Crush, omit the Cointreau and substitute $2^1/_2$ cups chilled lemon-lime soda for the vodka.

PIMM'S AT PLAY

This traditional English summertime drink with deep, complex flavors is perfect for tennis parties, polo matches, or any old backyard happening. An old British standard, Pimm's, a gin-based product made with aromatic herbs and lemonade, available in liquor stores, is making increasing waves in the States. Serve this punch at your next summer soiree and your friends will think you are definitely "of the moment."

Punch bowl and glasses
24 ice cubes made with maraschino cherries (see page 92)
3 cups Pimm's
3 cups chilled ginger ale
3 cups chilled lemon-lime soda
4 cups ice cubes
Lemon slices for garnish

At least 3 hours ahead, make the cherry ice cubes.

Combine the liquid ingredients in the punch bowl and mix well. Add the cherry and plain ice cubes. Garnish with the lemon slices and serve immediately.

SERVES 10

TROPICAL PARADISE

These tasty recipes all got their start on some stretch of tropical land. I've been inventive and added my own fun twist to these thirst quenchers, with the help of, of course, my indispensable taste-testing team. Create your own little piece of tropical paradise by mixing up a tantalizing batch of one, or all, of these punches.

Tequila and rum, favorites of the sultry climes, are the stars here, supported by a cast of fruit flavors including banana, coconut, cherry, blackberry, mango, guava, and virtually every citrus under the sun. Inventiveness was the focus when creating these tantalizing punches.

MARGARITA MADNESS

When you can't get to Margaritaville, I suggest whipping up a bowl of this feel-good-immediately concoction. The pear nectar brings a nice sweetness to the punch, balancing the tart lime. I find that serving these makes for a great party anytime, even during the winter months, as drinking one of these seems to melt the cold away. The traditional salting of the rims of the glasses is entirely optional, but I find it does enhance the sweet-and-sour taste experience.

Punch bowl and glasses
3 cups premium 100 percent agave silver tequila
2 cups pear nectar or juice
1 cup fresh lime juice
1 cup Cointreau
$^1/_2$ cup Grand Marnier
3 limes, thinly sliced
6 cups crushed ice
Coarse salt for glass rims (optional)

Combine the tequila, pear nectar, lime juice, Cointreau, and Grand Marnier in the punch bowl and mix well. Place the lime slices around the rim of the bowl for guests to help themselves to. Add the crushed ice to the punch. Serve immediately with a shallow dish of coarse salt for dipping the rims of the glasses, if desired, instructing guests to moisten the rim of their glass with a lime slice before dipping.

SERVES 12

✱ For nonalcoholic Margarita Madness, substitute 1 $^1/_2$ cups orange juice for the Cointreau and Grand Marnier, and omit the tequila.

CITRUS COOLER

This light and tangy concoction makes a great hot-weather antidote, as the zesty citrus seems to work magically to lower body temperatures immediately. Served after a sweltering summer day for a Manhattan rooftop soiree, this punch was a chilling success.

Punch bowl and glasses
2 cups light rum
2 cups tangerine juice
1 cup grapefruit juice
1/2 cup Cointreau
1/2 cup fresh lime juice
1/2 cup fresh lemon juice
1/4 cup cherry juice
6 cups ice cubes
Lemon and lime slices for garnish

Combine the liquid ingredients in the punch bowl and mix well. Add the ice cubes, garnish with the slices of lemon and lime, and serve immediately.

SERVES 10

✳ For a nonalcoholic Citrus Cooler, omit the Cointreau and substitute 2 cups tangerine juice for the rum.

DOCKSIDE DELIGHT

Too many of these and you'll miss the boat for sure. Or if you're cruising, be sure to watch for sandbars. The rum mixes swimmingly with the fruit juices, crème de banane, and the subtle blackberry flavor. Ahoy, matey!

Punch bowl and glasses
4 cups cranberry juice
3 cups pineapple juice
1 cup light rum
1 cup dark rum
$1/_2$ cup crème de banane
$1/_2$ cup cherry juice
$1/_2$ cup blackberry brandy
6 cups ice cubes
Maraschino cherries and fresh or drained canned pineapple chunks for garnish

Combine the liquid ingredients in the punch bowl and mix well. Add the ice cubes, garnish with the cherries and pineapple, and serve immediately.

SERVES 10

PARADISE FOUND

You can feel the tropical breezes sighing amid the palms whenever this punch is served. Play island tunes and transport your guests in mind, body, and spirit to a balmy evening on a white-sand beach.

Punch bowl and glasses
4 cups pineapple juice
2 cups orange juice
2 cups premium 100 percent agave silver tequila
$^3/_4$ cup blackberry brandy
$^1/_2$ cup grenadine
$^1/_2$ cup fresh lime juice
$^1/_4$ cup cream of coconut (see Note, page 27)
6 cups ice cubes

Combine the liquid ingredients in the punch bowl and mix well. Add the ice cubes and serve immediately.

SERVES 12

* For a nonalcoholic Paradise Found, substitute an additional 2 cups pineapple juice for the tequila and $^3/_4$ cup mixed berry juice for the blackberry brandy.

MANGO TANGO

A winning combination of tropical fruit juices and rum, the name of this punch alone adds instant zing to any gathering. It pairs perfectly with quesadillas or tortilla chips and spicy salsa. If you don't have time to make the ice form, add a few cups of ice cubes and the cubed fruit on its own.

Punch bowl and glasses
Ice form(s) made with fresh mango cubes
 and fresh or drained canned pineapple chunks (see page 92)
4 cups mango nectar or juice
2 cups pineapple juice
2 cups dark rum
1 cup light rum
1 cup guava nectar or juice
1 cup apricot juice
1/2 cup fresh lime juice
Lime slices for garnish

At least 3 hours ahead, make the ice form(s).

Combine the liquid ingredients in the punch bowl and mix well. Add the ice form(s) and lime slices and serve immediately.

SERVES 12

CHAMPAGNE WISHES

Ahh, but why not . . . the English do it at lunch on Saturdays, the French can't live without it. So let's do it. Let's drink Champagne. To balance the sweet fruit syrups and other ingredients called for in these punch recipes, be sure to use a Champagne that is both dry and crisp.

BUBBLING TIPS

Always have one good bottle of Champagne in your fridge for the impromptu toast. Or maybe you just feel like some bubbles to wash away your ridiculously long and stressful day.

Sunlight speeds up the fermentation process, so store Champagne on its side in the refrigerator or in a cool, dark place.

Always add Champagne last to the punch and stir just enough to blend. Stir very gently, as too much movement will cause the Champagne to lose its bubbles (gasp!).

PEACHY PASSIONS

This Champagne and peach combination is a twist to the classic Bellini. Originally created in Harry's Bar in Venice, the Bellini's two ingredients are peach puree and Champagne. In Peach Passions, we embrace the peach flavors and add a touch of citrus with the Cointreau.

Punch bowl and glasses
Ice form(s) made with rose blossoms and petals (see page 92)
1 cup brandy
1 cup fresh peach puree or nectar
$^1/_2$ cup Cointreau
1 $^1/_2$ cups chilled sparkling water
One bottle (750 ml) chilled dry Champagne

At least 3 hours ahead, make the ice form(s).

Combine the brandy, peach puree, and Cointreau in the punch bowl and mix well. Just before serving, slowly pour in the sparkling water and Champagne. Place the ice form(s) in the punch and serve immediately.

SERVES 8

PINK LADY PUNCH

*This punch got its name from its repeated appearance at numerous girlfriends'
gatherings. The smooth guava flavor comes alive when mixed with Champagne,
and the apricot adds another great layer of flavor. It's super-easy to mix up, looks
pretty, and puts everyone in a flirty mood. The bowl empties quickly with this popular
mix, so be sure to have extra ingredients on hand.*

Punch bowl and glasses
Ice form(s) made with citrus slices (see page 92)
2 cups guava nectar or juice
$^1/_2$ cup apricot brandy
Two bottles (750 ml each) chilled dry Champagne
Fresh raspberries for garnish

At least 3 hours ahead, make the ice form(s).

Combine the guava nectar and brandy in the punch bowl. Just before serving,
slowly pour in the Champagne. Place the ice form(s) in the punch, garnish
with raspberries, and serve immediately.

SERVES 8

FRUITY BUBBLES

The fresh juices mix perfectly with the distilled sweetness of the black currant liqueur and the Champagne adds the right touch of effervescence to the punch, perfect for mixing up some happy-hour fun or for a birthday celebration.

Punch bowl and glasses
1 cup crème de cassis (black currant liqueur)
1 cup cranberry juice
$1/4$ cup fresh lime juice
Two bottles (750 ml each) chilled dry Champagne
4 cups ice cubes
Fresh raspberries and/or blackberries for garnish (optional)

Combine the crème de cassis, cranberry juice, and lime juice in the punch bowl and mix well. Just before serving, slowly pour in the Champagne. Add the ice cubes, garnish with the berries, if using, and serve immediately.

SERVES 8

TANGERINE DREAMS

Here's a flavorful punch for the nondrinkers and pregnant ladies in the crowd—an essential option for gatherings served alongside Pink Lady Punch (page 67) or Afternoon Delight (page 72).

Punch bowl and Champagne glasses
Ice form(s) made with maraschino cherries (see page 92)
3 cups tangerine juice
1 cup pink grapefruit juice
1 cup white grapefruit juice
$1/_4$ cup cherry juice
8 cups chilled orange-flavored sparkling water

At least 3 hours ahead, make the ice form(s).

Combine the fruit juices in the punch bowl and mix well. Just before serving, slowly pour in the sparkling water. Place the ice forms in the punch and serve immediately.

SERVES 8

AFTERNOON DELIGHT

Pink grapefruit juice gives this punch great color and sweetness, while the pear nectar balances it, adding smoothness. Great as a morning concoction, here's a huge brunch favorite.

Punch bowl and glasses
24 ice cubes made with rose petals (see page 92)
2 cups pink grapefruit juice
2 cups pear nectar or juice
Two bottles (750 ml each) chilled dry Champagne

At least 3 hours ahead, make the ice cubes.

Combine the grapefruit juice and pear nectar in the punch bowl and mix well. Just before serving, slowly pour in the Champagne. Add the ice cubes and serve immediately.

SERVES 8

MIMOSA PUNCH

The age-old mimosa has become predictable and a bit boring. I set out to make it fun again. I entrusted a few willing tasters and landed on this reinvigorated version that's as easy to make as it is to drink! Here, mandarin orange juice is substituted for the old standard, but if you can't find mandarin, try blood orange or tangerine juice.

Punch bowl and stemmed glasses
2 cups mandarin orange juice
2 cups pear nectar or juice
$^1/_2$ cup Cointreau
Two bottles (750 ml each) chilled dry Champagne
2 cups ice cubes
Orange slices and fresh sliced strawberries for garnish

Combine the orange juice, pear nectar, and Cointreau in the punch bowl and mix well. Just before serving, slowly pour in the Champagne. Add the ice cubes, garnish with the orange and strawberry slices, and serve immediately.

SERVES 8

LOVE TRAIN

This sophisticated punch is a great addition to a festive Valentine's Day celebration. For a romantic evening for two, cut the recipe in half (or reduce it further, but no sense in letting any Champagne go to waste!).

Punch bowl and Champagne glasses
Ice form(s) made with fresh blackberries (see page 92)
1 cup crème de cassis (black currant liqueur)
$^1/_2$ cup Grand Marnier
Two bottles (750 ml each) chilled dry Champagne
Fresh blackberries for garnish

At least 3 hours ahead, make the ice form(s).

Combine the crème de cassis and Grand Marnier in the punch bowl and mix well. Just before serving, slowly pour in the Champagne. Place the ice form(s) in the punch, garnish with the blackberries, and serve immediately.

SERVES 8

COFFEE, TEA & LEMONADE

Since coffee and tea are always in demand when entertaining, why not innovate and serve them up in a delicious punch? The plethora of flavored teas available today make it far more interesting to brew. And like the standard beverages here, lemonade is a drink for all ages, from the classic to the sparkling. This chapter offers nonalcoholic mixes both rich and light. Of course, you can always spike it if you like!

COFFEE ON THE CUBES

This potent punch is coffee and dessert in one. Serve with biscotti for dipping and pass additional whipped cream for extra indulgence. For a fifth dimension, pour in a dash of your favorite flavored syrup such as hazelnut, almond, or mint. Flavored syrups are available in the coffee aisle at well-stocked grocery stores or in specialty-food markets.

Punch bowl and glasses
$2^1/_4$ **cups** light cream
$1^1/_2$ **cups** heavy cream
9 cups brewed coffee, cooled

2 tablespoons vanilla extract
6 ounces dark chocolate,
   grated on the large holes
   of a handheld grater

Fill ice cube trays with 2 cups of the light cream and freeze until solid, $2^1/_2$ to 3 hours.

In a small bowl using a whisk or an electric mixer, whip the heavy cream until soft peaks form. Set aside.

Combine the coffee, remaining $^1/_4$ cup light cream, and vanilla in the punch bowl and mix well. Add the cream ice cubes. Dollop the whipped cream on top of the coffee mixture and sprinkle the chocolate shavings on top. Serve immediately.

SERVES 10

✳ For spiked Coffee on the Cubes, substitute 1 cup Kahlúa for 1 cup of the brewed coffee.

> **NOTE:** *The whipped cream and chocolate shavings can be served next to the punch bowl in small bowls for guests to garnish their individual glasses.*

ROSE HIP AND HIBISCUS TEA PUNCH

A favorite with the shower set, this recipe always receives requests for copies from friends and family. The lemon juice mellows the intense tea flavor combination, while the orange juice adds just the right amount of sweetness. Tea bags are readily available with the rose hip and hibiscus combination; look for them in the coffee and tea aisle in any well-stocked grocery store.

Punch bowl and glasses
12 cups water
9 rose hip–hibiscus tea bags
¹/₄ cup sugar
1 cup fresh lemon juice
1 cup orange juice
6 cups ice cubes
Orange and lemon slices for garnish
Pesticide-free rose petals for garnish (see page 11)

In a large saucepan, bring the water to a boil. Remove from the heat and add the tea bags. Let steep for 10 minutes. Remove the tea bags and stir in the sugar until dissolved. Cover and refrigerate until chilled, about 1 hour.

To serve, pour the tea into the punch bowl. Add the lemon and orange juices and mix well. Add the ice cubes, fruit slices, and rose petals and serve immediately.

SERVES 10

GINGER TEA PUNCH

This blend of iced tea, ginger ale, and fresh ginger makes a splashingly refreshing drink on a sun-drenched summer day. I recently served it at a birthday party and got an enthusiastic reaction. Not only is ginger supposed to be good for you in all sorts of ways, it has a decidedly cooling effect in the summer.

Pitcher and glasses
10 cups water
10 bags black tea, such as orange pekoe
1 1/2-inch piece fresh gingerroot, peeled and thinly sliced
   (approximately 10 slices)
1/4 cup sugar
3 cups chilled ginger ale
6 cups ice cubes
Mint sprigs for garnish

In a large saucepan, bring the water to a boil. Remove from the heat and add the tea bags and gingerroot. Let steep for 10 minutes. Remove the tea bags and ginger. Stir in the sugar until dissolved. Cover and refrigerate until chilled, about 1 hour.

To serve, pour the tea into the pitcher. Slowly pour in the ginger ale. Add the ice cubes, garnish with the mint sprigs, and serve immediately.

SERVES 10

FRUITED TEA PUNCH

You can use whatever fruits are in peak season for this light and refreshing tea. It makes a great summertime drink, perfect for picnics, family reunions, or casual warm-weather gatherings.

Large sun tea jar or punch bowl and glasses
12 cups water
4 lemon-flavored tea bags
4 orange-flavored tea bags
1/2 cup sugar
6 cups ice cubes
1 orange, thinly sliced
1 nectarine, pitted and cut into small wedges
1 peach, pitted and cut into small wedges

In a large saucepan, bring the water to a boil. Remove from the heat and add the tea bags. Let steep for 10 minutes. Remove the tea bags. Stir in the sugar until dissolved. Refrigerate until chilled, about 1 hour.

To serve, pour the tea into the tea jar. Add the ice cubes and fruit slices and serve immediately.

SERVES 10

✻ For spiked Fruited Tea Punch, add 2 cups bourbon just before serving.

OLD-FASHIONED LEMONADE

A true classic refreshment, lemonade reminds me of my childhood summer days spent manning my stand at the end of the driveway, awaiting thirsty customers. Lemons vary in sweetness, so always taste and add more juice or Simple Syrup as needed for the desired balance.

Large sun tea jar, punch bowl, or pitcher with glasses
1 cup Simple Syrup (page 93), cooled
2 cups fresh lemon juice
8 cups cold water
6 cups ice cubes
Lemon slices for garnish

Combine the Simple Syrup, lemon juice, and water in the tea jar and mix well. Add the ice cubes, garnish with the lemon slices, and serve (or sell!).

SERVES 10

SPARKLING MINT AND STRAWBERRY LEMONADE

In this unusual twist on an old-fashioned favorite, strawberries supply a stunning color and lusciousness, while sparkling water adds bubbling delight. If you want even more color drama, add a dash of grenadine to heighten the effect.

Punch bowl or pitcher and glasses
3 cups fresh strawberries, hulled and quartered,
   plus a sliced strawberry or two for garnish
2 tablespoons chopped fresh mint leaves, plus mint sprigs for garnish
1 cup fresh lemon juice
1 cup Simple Syrup (page 93), cooled
4 cups chilled sparkling water
6 cups ice cubes

In a blender or food processor, combine the strawberries and mint leaves and process to a puree. Strain the puree through a fine-mesh sieve. Transfer to the punch bowl. Add the lemon juice and Simple Syrup and mix well. Just before serving, slowly pour in the sparkling water. Add the ice cubes, garnish with the sliced strawberries and mint sprigs, and serve immediately.

SERVES 8

BASIC RECIPES

DECORATIVE ICE CUBES

As a general guideline, use 6 cups of ice cubes (about 3 trays) to chill 8 to 12 servings of punch. Make sure the trays are clean before using for decorative ice.

Fill the trays halfway with water. Place one decorative item such as a flower petal (see page 11), berry, or herb leaf in each section of the tray. Freeze for 30 minutes or so to set. Remove the trays from the freezer and fill to the top with water. Return to the freezer until frozen solid, 2 to 3 hours.

When ready to serve, remove the trays from the freezer and run under warm water while gently tapping on the trays to dislodge the ice. Add to the punch immediately.

DECORATIVE ICE RINGS AND OTHER FORMS

As a general guideline, use one 8-inch ring or other mold or two or three 4-inch or smaller molds to chill 8 to 12 servings of punch. Make sure the molds are clean before using. Fill the mold(s) halfway with water. Add the decorative ingredients such as flower petals or blossoms (see page 11), fruits, berries, or herbs and arrange them in a pleasing pattern. Freeze for 30 minutes or so to set. Remove the mold(s) from the freezer and fill to the top with water. Return to the freezer until frozen solid, 2 to 3 hours.

When ready to serve, remove the mold(s) from the freezer and run under warm water while gently tapping on the mold(s) to dislodge the ice. Add to the punch immediately.

SIMPLE SYRUP

Simple Syrup is a key ingredient in many punch recipes, as a sweetener that incorporates easily. It takes just a few minutes to whip up. Always add a little bit of Simple Syrup at a time, tasting as you go, as fruits and fruit juices, concentrates, and nectars have varying sugar contents and the punch may need less syrup than the recipe calls for.

To make Simple Syrup, combine 1 cup water and 1 cup sugar in a saucepan and bring to a boil. Stir constantly until the sugar has dissolved and the liquid is clear, about 5 minutes. Remove from the heat and let cool. The syrup will keep, refrigerated in a sealed jar or container, for up to 1 week. **MAKES 1 CUP**

Variations

For mint-flavored Simple Syrup, make the simple syrup as directed. When removed from the heat, stir in 1 cup loosely packed fresh mint leaves. Let steep for 15 minutes. Strain the syrup and discard the mint. Alternatively, to make other flavored syrups, add 2 teaspoons extract such as lemon, orange, vanilla, or almond to the cooled Simple Syrup.

NOTE: To make more or less syrup, combine equal parts sugar and water and proceed as directed.

RASPBERRY PUREE

In a blender, process 4 cups of fresh or frozen raspberries to a smooth puree. Strain the puree into a bowl through a fine-mesh sieve to remove the seeds, pushing on the mixture with the back of a wooden spoon to extract all the juice. Refrigerate until chilled or add to the punch immediately. The puree will keep, covered and refrigerated, for up to 2 days.

INDEX

Afternoon Delight, 72

Bloody Mary Bowl, 32
Bourbon
    Fruited Tea Punch, 87
    Holiday Ho Ho, 36
    Julep Jubilee, 43
    Mulled Cider, 39
Bowls, 10
Brandy, 8
    Dockside Delight, 56
    Gin Rummy, 40
    Holiday Ho Ho, 36
    Paradise Found, 59
    Peachy Passions, 64
    Pink Lady Punch, 67
    Sunrise Surprise, 24

Champagne, 63
    Afternoon Delight, 72
    Fruity Bubbles, 68
    Love Train, 76
    Mimosa Punch, 75
    Peachy Passions, 64
    Pink Lady Punch, 67
Cider, Mulled, 39
Citrus Cooler, 55
Coconut, cream of, 27
Coffee on the Cubes, 80
Cointreau
    Citrus Cooler, 55
    Margarita Madness, 52
    Mimosa Punch, 75
    Orange Crush, 47

Peachy Passions, 64
Sassy Sangria, 35
Sunrise Surprise, 24
Cranberry juice
    Dockside Delight, 56
    Fruity Bubbles, 68
    Nantucket Lemonade, 16
    Petal Punch, 20
Crème de banane
    Dockside Delight, 56
Crème de cassis
    Fruity Bubbles, 68
    Love Train, 76

Dockside Delight, 56

Egg nog
    Holiday Ho Ho, 36

Flowers, 11
Fruits, 11, 15. See also
individual fruits
    Fruited Tea Punch, 87
    Fruit Smoothie, 19
    Fruity Bubbles, 68

Garnishes, 11
Gin, 8
    Gin Rummy, 40
Ginger ale
    Ginger Tea Punch, 84
    Pimm's at Play, 48

Glasses, 10–11
Grand Marnier
    Love Train, 76
    Margarita Madness, 52
Grapefruit juice
    Afternoon Delight, 72
    Citrus Cooler, 55
    Tangerine Dreams, 71
Grenadine
    Paradise Found, 59
Guava nectar
    Mango Tango, 60
    Pink Lady Punch, 67

Herbs, 11
History, 7
Holiday Ho Ho, 36

Ice, decorative, 12, 92

Julep Jubilee, 43

Kahlúa
    Coffee on the Cubes, 80

Ladles, 11
Lemonade
    Nantucket Lemonade, 16
    Old-Fashioned Lemonade, 88
    Sparkling Mint and
    Strawberry Lemonade, 91

94

Limes
    Margarita Madness, 52
    Minty Mojito, 44
Liqueurs, 8–9. *See also individual liqueurs*
Love Train, 76

Mango nectar
    Mango Tango, 60
    Sunrise Surprise, 24
Margarita Madness, 52
Melon Melody, 27
Mimosa Punch, 75
Mint, 11
    Julep Jubilee, 43
    Minty Mojito, 44
    Sparkling Mint and
        Strawberry Lemonade, 91
Mojito, Minty, 44
Mulled Cider, 39

Nantucket Lemonade, 16

Old-Fashioned Lemonade, 88
Oranges
    Mimosa Punch, 75
    Orange Crush, 47

Papaya Pleaser, 28
Paradise Found, 59
Passion fruit juice
    Sunrise Surprise, 24

Peachy Passions, 64
Pear nectar
    Afternoon Delight, 72
    Margarita Madness, 52
    Mimosa Punch, 75
Petal Punch, 20
Pimm's at Play, 48
Pineapple juice
    Dockside Delight, 56
    Fruit Smoothie, 19
    Mango Tango, 60
    Melon Melody, 27
    Paradise Found, 59
    Raspberry Rambler, 23
    Sunrise Surprise, 24
Pink Lady Punch, 67

Raspberries
    Fruit Smoothie, 19
    Raspberry Puree, 93
    Raspberry Rambler, 23
Rose Hip and Hibiscus
    Tea Punch, 83
Rum, 9, 19
    Citrus Cooler, 55
    Dockside Delight, 56
    Fruit Smoothie, 19
    Mango Tango, 60
    Minty Mojito, 44
    Papaya Pleaser, 28
    Sunrise Surprise, 24

Sangria, Sassy, 35
Simple Syrup, 93

Strawberry and Mint
    Lemonade, Sparkling, 91
Sunrise Surprise, 24

Tangerine juice
    Citrus Cooler, 55
    Tangerine Dreams, 71
Tea
    Fruited Tea Punch, 87
    Ginger Tea Punch, 84
    Rose Hip and Hibiscus
        Tea Punch, 83
Tequila, 9
    Margarita Madness, 52
    Paradise Found, 59
Tips, 13
Tomato juice
    Bloody Mary Bowl, 32
    Virgin Mary Bowl, 32

Virgin Mary Bowl, 32
Vodka, 9
    Bloody Mary Bowl, 32
    Melon Melody, 27
    Nantucket Lemonade, 16
    Orange Crush, 47
    Raspberry Rambler, 23

Whisky, 9. *See also* Bourbon
Wine. *See also* Champagne
    Petal Punch, 20
    Sassy Sangria, 35

TABLE OF EQUIVALENTS

The exact equivalents in the following tables have been rounded for convenience.

LIQUID/DRY MEASURES

U.S.	METRIC
$1/4$ teaspoon	1.25 milliliters
$1/2$ teaspoon	2.5 milliliters
1 teaspoon	5 milliliters
1 tablespoon (3 teaspoons)	15 milliliters
1 fluid ounce (2 tablespoons)	30 milliliters
$1/4$ cup	60 milliliters
$1/3$ cup	80 milliliters
$1/2$ cup	120 milliliters
1 cup	240 milliliters
1 pint (2 cups)	480 milliliters
1 quart (4 cups, 32 ounces)	960 milliliters
1 gallon (4 quarts)	3.84 liters
1 ounce (by weight)	28 grams
1 pound	454 grams
2.2 pounds	1 kilogram

LENGTH

U.S.	METRIC
$1/8$ inch	3 millimeters
$1/4$ inch	6 millimeters
$1/2$ inch	12 millimeters
1 inch	2.5 centimeters

OVEN TEMPERATURE

FAHRENHEIT	CELSIUS	GAS
250	120	$1/2$
275	140	1
300	150	2
325	160	3
350	180	4
375	190	5
400	200	6
425	220	7
450	230	8
475	240	9
500	260	10